The Constitution of
The State of Iowa:
A Quick Reference Guide

Bootblack Budget Books
Copyright 2018 ©
ISBN-13: 978-1986160049
ISBN-10: 1986160041

Contents:

Preamble and Boundaries – Page 19

Article I: Bill of Rights – Page 20

Section 1. Rights of Persons

Section 2. Political Power

Section 3. Religion

Section 4. Religious Test — Witnesses

Section 5. Dueling. Repealed

Section 6. Laws Uniform

Section 7. Liberty Of Speech and Press

Section 8. Personal Security — Searches and Seizures

Section 9. Right of Trial By Jury — Due Process of Law

Section 10. Rights of Persons Accused

Section 11. When Indictment Necessary — Grand Jury

Section 12. Twice Tried — Bail

Section 13. Habeas Corpus

Section 14. Military

Section 15. Quartering Soldiers

Section 16. Treason

Section 17. Bail — Punishments

Section 18. Eminent Domain — Drainage Ditches and Levees

Section 19. Imprisonment for Debt

Section 20. Right of Assemblage — Petition

Section 21. Attainder — Ex Post Facto Law — Obligation of Contract

Section 22. Resident Aliens

Section 23. Slavery — Penal Servitude

Section 24. Agricultural Leases

Section 25. Rights Reserved

Article II: Rights of Suffrage – Page 26

Section 1. Electors

Section 2. Privileged from Arrest

Section 3. From Military Duty

Section 4. Persons in Military Service

Section 5. Disqualified Persons

Section 6. Ballot

Section 7. General Election

Article III: Distribution of Powers – Page 28

Section 1. Departments of Government

Legislative Department

Section 1. General Assembly

Section 2. Annual Sessions of General Assembly — Special Sessions

Section 3. Representatives

Section 4. Qualifications

Section 5. Senators — Qualifications

Section 6. Senators — Number and Classification

Section 7. Officers — Elections Determined

Section 8. Quorum

Section 9. Authority of The Houses

Section 10. Protest — Record of Vote

Section 11. Privileged from Arrest

Section 12. Vacancies

Section 13. Doors Open

Section 14. Adjournments

Section 15. Bills

Section 16. Executive Approval — Veto — Item Veto by Governor

Section 17. Passage of Bills

Section 18. Receipts and Expenditures

Section 19. Impeachment

Section 20. Officers Subject to Impeachment — Judgment

Section 21. Members not Appointed to Office

Section 22. Disqualification

Section 23. Failure to Account

Section 24. Appropriations

Section 25. Compensation and Expenses of General Assembly

Section 26. Time Laws to Take Effect

Section 27. Divorce

Section 28. Lotteries. Repealed

Section 29. Acts—One Subject—Expressed in Title

Section 30. Local or Special Laws — General and Uniform — Boundaries of Counties

Section 31. Extra Compensation — Payment of Claims — Appropriations for Local or Private Purposes

Section 32. Oath of Members

Section 33. Census. Repealed

Section 34. Senate and House of Representatives — Limitation

Section 35. Senators and Representatives — Number and Districts

Section 36. Review by Supreme Court

Section 37. Congressional Districts

Section 38. Elections by General Assembly

Section 38a. Municipal Home Rule

Section 39. Legislative Districts

Section 39a. Counties Home Rule

Section 40. Nullification of Administrative Rules

Article IV: Executive Department – Page 40

Section 1. Governor

Section 2. Election and Term

Section 3. Governor and Lieutenant Governor Elected Jointly — Returns of Elections

Section 4. Election by General Assembly in Case of Tie — Succession by Lieutenant Governor

Section 5. Contested Elections

Section 6. Eligibility

Section 7. Commander in Chief

Section 8. Duties Of Governor

Section 9. Execution Of Laws

Section 10. Vacancies

Section 11. Convening General Assembly

Section 12. Message

Section 13. Adjournment

Section 14. Disqualification

Section 15. Terms — Compensation

Section 16. Pardons — Reprieves — Commutations

Section 17. Lieutenant Governor to Act as Governor

Section 18. Duties of Lieutenant Governor

Section 19. Succession to Office of Governor and Lieutenant Governor

Section 20. Seal of State

Section 21. Grants and Commissions

Section 22. Secretary — Auditor — Treasurer

Article V: Judicial Department – Page 46

Section 1. Courts

Section 2. Supreme Court

Section 3. Election of Judges — Term. Repealed

Section 4. Jurisdiction of Supreme Court

Section 5. District Court and Judge. Repealed

Section 6. Jurisdiction of District Court

Section 7. Conservators of the Peace

Section 8. Style of Process

Section 9. Salaries. Repealed

Section 10. Judicial Districts

Section 11. Judges — When Chosen. Repealed

Section 12. Attorney General

Section 13. District Attorney. Repealed

Section 14. System of Court Practice

Section 15. Vacancies in Courts

Section 16. State and District Nominating Commissions

Section 17. Terms — Judicial Elections

Section 18. Salaries — Qualifications — Retirement

Section 19. Retirement and Discipline of Judges

Article VI: Militia – Page 52

Section 1. Composition — Training

Section 2. Exemption

Section 3. Officers

Article VII: State Debts – Page 53

Section 1. Credit not to be Loaned

Section 2. Limitation

Section 3. Losses to School Funds

Section 4. War Debts

Section 5. Contracting Debt — Submission to the People

Section 6. Legislature May Repeal

Section 7. Tax Imposed Distinctly Stated

Section 8. Motor Vehicle Fees and Fuel Taxes

Section 9. Fish and Wildlife Protection Funds

Section 10. Natural Resources

Article VIII: Corporations – Page 57

Section 1. How Created

Section 2. Taxation of Corporations

Section 3. State not to be a Stockholder

Section 4. Municipal Corporations

Section 5. Banking Associations

Section 6. State Bank

Section 7. Specie Basis

Section 8. General Banking Law

Section 9. Stockholders Responsibility

Section 10. Billholders Preferred

Section 11. Speciepayments—Suspension

Section 12. Amendment or Repeal of Laws — Exclusive Privileges

Article IX: Education and School Lands — Page 60

Part 1: Education and School Lands

Section 1. Board of Education. Omitted

Section 2. Eligibility. Omitted

Section 3. Election Of Members. Omitted

Section 4. First Session. Omitted

Section 5. Limitation of Sessions. Omitted

Section 6. Secretary. Omitted

Section 7. Rules and Regulations. Omitted

Section 8. Power to Legislate. Omitted

Section 9. Governor Ex Officio a Member. Omitted

Section 10. Expenses. Omitted

Section 11. State University. Omitted

Section 12. Common Schools. Omitted

Section 13. Compensation. Omitted

Section 14. Quorum — Style of Acts. Omitted

Section 15. Board may be Abolished

Part 2: School Funds and School Lands

Section 1. Control — Management

Section 2. Permanent Fund

Section 3. Perpetual Support Fund

Section 4. Fines — How Appropriated. Repealed

Section 5. Proceeds of Lands

Section 6. Agents of School Funds

Section 7. Distribution. Repealed

Article X: Amendments to the Constitution – Page 65

Section 1. How Proposed — Submission

Section 2. More Than One Amendment

Section 3. Constitutional Convention

Article XI: Miscellaneous – Page 67

Section 1. Justice of Peace — Jurisdiction

Section 2. Counties

Section 3. Indebtedness of Political or Municipal Corporations

Section 4. Boundaries of State

Section 5. Oath of Office

Section 6. How Vacancies Filled

Section 7. Land Grants Located

Section 8. Seat of Government Established — State University

Article XII: Schedule – Page 69

Section 1. Supreme Law — Constitutionality of Acts

Section 2. Laws in Force

Section 3. Proceedings not Affected. Omitted

Section 4. Fines Inure to the State. Repealed

Section 5. Bonds in Force. Omitted

Section 6. First Election for Governor and Lieutenant Governor. Omitted

Section 7. First Election of Officers. Omitted

Section 8. For Judges of Supreme Court. Omitted

Section 9. General Assembly — First Session. Omitted

Preamble:

WE THE PEOPLE OF THE STATE OF IOWA, grateful to the Supreme Being for the blessings hitherto enjoyed, and feeling our dependence on Him for a continuation of those blessings, do ordain and establish a free and independent government, by the name of the State of Iowa, the boundaries whereof shall be as follows:

Boundaries:

Beginning in the middle of the main channel of the Mississippi River, at a point due East of the middle of the mouth of the main channel of the Des Moines River, thence up the middle of the main channel of the said Des Moines River, to a point on said river where the Northern boundary line of the State of Missouri-- as established by the constitution of that State--adopted June 12th, 1820--crosses the said middle of the main channel of the said Des Moines River; thence Westwardly along the said Northern boundary line of the State of Missouri, as established at the time aforesaid, until an extension of said line intersects the middle of the main channel of the Missouri River; thence up the middle of the main channel of the said Missouri River to a point opposite the middle of the main channel of the Big Sioux River, according to Nicollett's Map; thence up the main channel of the said Big Sioux River, according to the said map, until it is intersected by the parallel of forty three degrees and thirty minutes North latitude; thence East along said parallel of forty three degrees and thirty minutes until said parallel intersects the middle of the main channel of the Mississippi River; thence down the middle of the main channel of said Mississippi River to the place of beginning.

ARTICLE I: BILL OF RIGHTS

Section 1. Rights of Persons

All men and women are, by nature, free and equal, and have certain inalienable rights--among which are those of enjoying and defending life and liberty, acquiring, possessing and protecting property, and pursuing and obtaining safety and happiness.

Section 2. Political Power

All political power is inherent in the people. Government is instituted for the protection, security, and benefit of the people, and they have the right, at all times, to alter or reform the same, whenever the public good may require it.

Section 3. Religion

The general assembly shall make no law respecting an establishment of religion, or prohibiting the free exercise thereof; nor shall any person be compelled to attend any place of worship, pay tithes, taxes, or other rates for building or repairing places of worship, or the maintenance of any minister, or ministry.

Section 4. Religious Test—Witnesses

No religious test shall be required as a qualification for any office, or public trust, and no person shall be deprived of any of his rights, privileges, or capacities, or disqualified from the performance of any of his public or private duties, or rendered incompetent to give evidence in any court of law or equity, in consequence of his opinions on the subject of religion; and any party to any judicial proceeding shall have the right to use as a witness, or take the testimony of, any other person not disqualified on account of interest, who may be cognizant of any fact material to the case; and parties to suits may be witnesses, as provided by law.

Section 5. Dueling Repealed

Section 6. Laws Uniform

All laws of a general nature shall have a uniform operation; the general assembly shall not grant to any citizen, or class of citizens, privileges or immunities, which, upon the same terms shall not equally belong to all citizens.

Section 7. Liberty of Speech and Press

Every person may speak, write, and publish his sentiments on all subjects, being responsible for the abuse of that right. No law shall be passed to restrain or abridge the liberty of speech, or of the press. In all prosecutions or indictments for libel, the truth may be given in evidence to the jury, and if it appears to the jury that the matter charged as libellous was true, and was published with good motives and for justifiable ends, the party shall be acquitted.

Section 8. Personal Security--Searches and Seizures

The right of the people to be secure in their persons, houses, papers and effects, against unreasonable seizures and searches shall not be violated; and no warrant shall issue but on probable cause, supported by oath or affirmation, particularly describing the place to be searched, and the persons and things to be seized.

Section 9. Right of Trial by Jury--Due Process of Law

The right of trial by jury shall remain inviolate; but the general assembly may authorize trial by a jury of a less number than twelve men in inferior courts; but no person shall be deprived of life, liberty, or property, without due process of law.

Section 10. Rights of Persons Accused

In all criminal prosecutions, and in cases involving the life, or liberty of an individual the accused shall have a right to a speedy and public trial by an impartial jury; to be informed of the accusation against him, to have a copy of the same when demanded; to be confronted with the witnesses against him; to have compulsory process for his witnesses; and, to have the assistance of counsel.

Section 11. When Indictment Necessary--Grand Jury

All offenses less than felony and in which the maximum permissible imprisonment does not exceed thirty days shall be tried summarily before an officer authorized by law, on information under oath, without indictment, or the intervention of a grand jury, saving to the defendant the right of appeal; and no person shall be held to answer for any higher criminal offense, unless on presentment or indictment by a grand jury, except in cases arising in the army, or navy, or in the militia, when in actual service, in time of war or public danger.
The grand jury may consist of any number of members not less than five, nor more than fifteen, as the general assembly may by law provide, or the general assembly may provide for holding persons to answer for any criminal offense without the intervention of a grand jury.

Section 12. Twice Tried—Bail

No person shall after acquittal, be tried for the same offense. All persons shall, before conviction, be bailable, by sufficient sureties, except for capital offenses where the proof is evident, or the presumption great.

Section 13. Habeas Corpus

The writ of habeas corpus shall not be suspended, or refused when application is made as required by law, unless in case of rebellion, or invasion the public safety may require it.

Section 14. Military

The military shall be subordinate to the civil power. No standing army shall be kept up by the state in time of peace; and in time of war, no appropriation for a standing army shall be for a longer time than two years.

Section 15. Quartering Soldiers

No soldier shall, in time of peace, be quartered in any house without the consent of the owner, nor in time of war except in the manner prescribed by law.

Section 16. Treason

Treason against the state shall consist only in levying war against it, adhering to its enemies, or giving them aid and comfort. No person shall be convicted of treason, unless on the evidence of two witnesses to the same overt act, or confession in open court.

Section 17. Bail—Punishments

Excessive bail shall not be required; excessive fines shall not be imposed, and cruel and unusual punishment shall not be inflicted.

Section 18. Eminent Domain

Private property shall not be taken for public use without just compensation first being made, or secured to be made to the owner thereof, as soon as the damages shall be assessed by a jury, who shall not take into consideration any advantages that may result to said owner on account of the improvement for which it is taken.

The general assembly, however, may pass laws permitting the owners of lands to construct drains, ditches, and levees for agricultural, sanitary or mining purposes across the lands of others, and provide for the organization of drainage districts, vest the proper authorities with power to construct and maintain levees, drains and ditches and to keep in repair all drains, ditches, and levees heretofore constructed under the laws of the state, by special assessments upon the property benefited thereby. The general assembly may provide by law for the condemnation of such real estate as shall be necessary for the construction and maintenance of such drains, ditches and levees, and prescribe the method of making such condemnation.

Section 19. Imprisonment for Debt

No person shall be imprisoned for debt in any civil action, on mesne or final process, unless in case of fraud; and no person shall be imprisoned for a militia fine in time of peace.

Section 20. Rights of Assemblage—Petition

The people have the right freely to assemble together to counsel for the common good; to make known their opinions to their representatives and to petition for a redress of grievances.

Section 21. Ex Post Facto Law--Obligation of Contract

No bill of attainder, ex post facto law, or law impairing the obligation of contracts, shall ever be passed.

Section 22. Resident Aliens

Foreigners who are, or may hereafter become residents of this state, shall enjoy the same rights in respect to the possession, enjoyment and descent of property, as native born citizens.

Section 23. Slavery--Penal Servitude

There shall be no slavery in this state; nor shall there be involuntary servitude, unless for the punishment of crime.

Section 24. Agricultural Leases

No lease or grant of agricultural lands, reserving any rent, or service of any kind, shall be valid for a longer period than twenty years.

Section 25. Rights Reserved

This enumeration of rights shall not be construed to impair or deny others, retained by the people.

ARTICLE II: RIGHTS OF SUFFRAGE

Section 1. Electors

Every citizen of the United States of the age of twenty-one years, who shall have been a resident of this state for such period of time as shall be provided by law and of the county in which he claims his vote for such period of time as shall be provided by law, shall be entitled to vote at all elections which are now or hereafter may be authorized by law. The general assembly may provide by law for different periods of residence in order to vote for various officers or in order to vote in various elections. The required periods of residence shall not exceed six months in this state and sixty days in the county.

Section 2. Privileged from Arrest

Electors shall, in all cases except treason, felony, or breach of the peace, be privileged from arrest on the days of election, during their attendance at such election, going to and returning therefrom.

Section 3. From Military Duty

No elector shall be obliged to perform military duty on the day of election, except in time of war, or public danger.

Section 4. Persons in Military Service

No person in the military, naval, or marine service of the United States shall be considered a resident of this state by being stationed in any garrison, barrack, or military or naval place, or station within this state.

Section 5. Disqualified Persons

A person adjudged mentally incompetent to vote or a person convicted of any infamous crime shall not be entitled to the privilege of an elector.

Section 6. Ballot

All elections by the people shall be by ballot.

Section 7. General Election

The general election for state, district, county and township officers in the year 1916 shall be held in the same month and on the same day as that fixed by the laws of the United States for the election of presidential electors, or of president and vice-president of the United States; and thereafter such election shall be held at such time as the general assembly may by law provide.

ARTICLE III: OF THE DISTRIBUTION OF POWERS

Section 1. Departments of Government

The powers of the government of Iowa shall be divided into three separate departments--the legislative, the executive, and the judicial: and no person charged with the exercise of powers properly belonging to one of these departments shall exercise any function appertaining to either of the others, except in cases hereinafter expressly directed or permitted.

THE LEGISLATIVE DEPARTMENT

Section 1. General Assembly

The legislative authority of this state shall be vested in a general assembly, which shall consist of a senate and house of representatives: and the style of every law shall be. "Be it enacted by the General Assembly of the State of Iowa."

Section 1. Annual Sessions of General Assembly--Special Sessions

The general assembly shall meet in session on the second Monday of January of each year. Upon written request to the presiding officer of each house of the general assembly by two-thirds of the members of each house, the general assembly shall convene in special session. The governor of the state may convene the general assembly by proclamation in the interim.

Section 3. Representatives

The members of the house of representatives shall be chosen every second year, by the qualified electors of their respective districts, [* * *]* and their term of office shall commence on the first day of January next after their election, and continue two years, and until their successors are elected and qualified.

Section 4. Qualifications

No person shall be a member of the house of representatives who shall not have attained the age of twenty-one years, be a citizen of the United States, and shall have been an inhabitant of this state one year next preceding his election, and at the time of his election shall have had an actual residence of sixty days in the county, or district he may have been chosen to represent.

Section 5. Senators—Qualifications

Senators shall be chosen for the term of four years, at the same time and place as representatives; they shall be twenty-five years of age, and possess the qualifications of representatives as to residence and citizenship.

Section 6. Senators--Number and Classifications

The number of senators shall total not more than one-half the membership of the house of representatives. Senators shall be classified so that as nearly as possible one-half of the members of the senate shall be elected every two years.

Section 7. Officers--Elections Determined

Each house shall choose its own officers, and judge of the qualification, election, and return of its own members. A contested election shall be determined in such manner as shall be directed by law.

Section 8. Quorum

A majority of each house shall constitute a quorum to transact business; but a smaller number may adjourn from day to day, and may compel the attendance of absent members in such manner and under such penalties as each house may provide.

Section 9. Authority of the Houses

Each house shall sit upon its own adjournments, keep a journal of its proceedings, and publish the same; determine its rules of proceedings, punish members for disorderly behavior, and, with the consent of two thirds, expel a member, but not a second time for the same offense; and shall have all other powers necessary for a branch of the general assembly of a free and independent state.

Section 10. Protest--Record of Vote

Every member of the general assembly shall have the liberty to dissent from, or protest against any act or resolution which he may think injurious to the public, or an individual, and have the reasons for his dissent entered on the journals; and the yeas and nays of the members of either house, on any question, shall, at the desire of any two members present, be entered on the journals.

Section 11. Privileged from Arrest

Senators and representatives, in all cases, except treason, felony, or breach of the peace, shall be privileged from arrest during the session of the general assembly, and in going to and returning from the same.

Section 12. Vacancies

When vacancies occur in either house, the governor or the person exercising the functions of governor, shall issue writs of election to fill such vacancies.

Section 13. Doors Open

The doors of each house shall be open, except on such occasions, as, in the opinion of the house, may require secrecy.

Section 14. Adjournments

Neither house shall, without the consent of the other, adjourn for more than three days, nor to any other place than that in which they may be sitting.

Section 15. Bills

Bills may originate in either house, and may be amended, altered, or rejected by the other; and every bill having passed both houses, shall be signed by the speaker and president of their respective houses.

Section 16. Executive Approval--Veto--Item Veto by Governor

Every bill which shall have passed the general assembly, shall, before it becomes a law, be presented to the governor. If he approve, he shall sign it; but if not, he shall return it with his objections, to the house in which it originated, which shall enter the same upon their journal, and proceed to reconsider it; if, after such reconsideration, it again pass both houses, by yeas and nays, by a majority of two thirds of the members of each house, it shall become a law, notwithstanding the governor's objections. If any bill shall not be returned within three days after it shall have been presented to him, Sunday excepted, the same shall be a law in like manner as if he had signed it, unless the general assembly, by adjournment, prevent such return. Any bill submitted to the governor for his approval during the last three days of a session of the general assembly, shall be deposited by him in the office of the secretary of state, within thirty days after the adjournment, with his approval, if approved by him, and with his objections, if he disapproves thereof.

The governor may approve appropriation bills in whole or in part, and may disapprove any item of an appropriation bill; and the part approved shall become a law. Any item of an appropriation bill disapproved by the governor shall be returned, with his objections, to the house in which it originated, or shall be deposited by him in the office of the secretary of state in the case of an appropriation bill submitted to the governor for his approval during the last three days of a session of the general assembly, and the procedure in each case shall be the same as provided for other bills. Any such item of an appropriation bill may be enacted into law notwithstanding the governor's objections, in the same manner as provided for other bills.

Section 17. Passage of Bills

No bill shall be passed unless by the assent of a majority of all the members elected to each branch of the general assembly, and the question upon the final passage shall be taken immediately upon its last reading, and the yeas and nays entered on the journal.

Section 18. Receipts and Expenditures

An accurate statement of the receipts and expenditures of the public money shall be attached to and published with the laws, at every regular session of the general assembly.

Section 19. Impeachment

The house of representatives shall have the sole power of impeachment, and all impeachments shall be tried by the senate. When sitting for that purpose, the senators shall be upon oath or affirmation; and no person shall be convicted without the concurrence of two thirds of the members present.

Section 20. Officers Subject to Impeachment—Judgment

The governor, judges of the supreme and district courts, and other state officers, shall be liable to impeachment for any misdemeanor or malfeasance in office; but judgment in such cases shall extend only to removal from office, and disqualification to hold any office of honor, trust, or profit, under this state; but the party convicted or acquitted shall nevertheless be liable to indictment, trial, and punishment, according to law. All other civil officers shall be tried for misdemeanors and malfeasance in office, in such manner as the general assembly may provide.

Section 21. Members Not Appointed to Office

No senator or representative shall, during the time for which he shall have been elected, be appointed to any civil office of profit under this state, which shall have been created, or the emoluments of which shall have been increased during such term, except such offices as may be filled by elections by the people.

Section 22. Disqualifications

No person holding any lucrative office under the United States, or this state, or any other power, shall be eligible to hold a seat in the general assembly; but offices in the militia, to which there is attached no annual salary, or the office of justice of the peace, or postmaster whose compensation does not exceed one hundred dollars per annum, or notary public, shall not be deemed lucrative.

Section 23. Failure to Account

No person who may hereafter be a collector or holder of public monies, shall have a seat in either house of the general assembly, or be eligible to hold any office of trust or profit in this state, until he shall have accounted for and paid into the treasury all sums for which he may be liable.

Section 24. Appropriations

No money shall be drawn from the treasury but in consequence of appropriations made by law.

Section 25. Compensation and Expenses of General Assembly

Each member of the general assembly shall receive such compensation and allowances for expenses as shall be fixed by law but no general assembly shall have the power to increase compensation and allowances effective prior to the convening of the next general assembly following the session in which any increase is adopted.

Section 26. Time Laws to Take Effect

An act of the general assembly passed at a regular session of a general assembly shall take effect on July 1 following its passage unless a different effective date is stated in an act of the general assembly. An act passed at a special session of a general assembly shall take effect ninety days after adjournment of the special session unless a different effective date is stated in an act of the general assembly. The general assembly may establish by law a procedure for giving notice of the contents of acts of immediate importance which become law.

Section 27. Divorce

No divorce shall be granted by the general assembly.

Section 28. Lotteries

Repealed

Section 29. Acts--One Subject--Expressed in Title

Every act shall embrace but one subject, and matters properly connected therewith; which subject shall be expressed in the title. But if any subject shall be embraced in an act which shall not be expressed in the title, such act shall be void only as to so much thereof as shall not be expressed in the title.

Section 30. Local or Special Laws--General and Uniform--Boundaries of Counties

The general assembly shall not pass local or special laws in the following cases: For the assessment and collection of taxes for state, county, or road purposes; For laying out, opening, and working roads or highways; For changing the names of persons; For the incorporation of cities and towns; For vacating roads, town plats, streets, alleys, or public squares; For locating or changing county seats.

In all the cases above enumerated, and in all other cases where a general law can be made applicable, all laws shall be general, and of uniform operation throughout the state; and no law changing the boundary lines of any county shall have effect until upon being submitted to the people of the counties affected by the change, at a general election, it shall be approved by a majority of the votes in each county, cast for and against it.

Section 31. Extra Compensation--Payment of Claims--Appropriations for Local or Private Purposes

No extra compensation shall be made to any officer, public agent, or contractor, after the service shall have been rendered, or the contract entered into; nor, shall any money be paid on any claim, the subject matter of which shall not have been provided for by preexisting laws, and no public money or property shall be appropriated for local, or private purposes, unless such appropriation, compensation, or claim, be allowed by two thirds of the members elected to each branch of the general assembly.

Section 32. Oath of Members

Members of the general assembly shall, before they enter upon the duties of their respective offices, take and subscribe the following oath or affirmation: "I do solemnly swear, or affirm, (as the case may be,) that I will support the Constitution of the United States, and the Constitution of the State of Iowa, and that

I will faithfully discharge the duties of senator, (or representative, as the case may be,) according to the best of my ability." And members of the general assembly are hereby empowered to administer to each other the said oath or affirmation.

Section 33. Census

Repealed

Section 34. Senate and House of Representatives—Limitation

The senate shall be composed of not more than fifty and the house of representatives of not more than one hundred members. Senators and representatives shall be elected from districts established by law. Each district so established shall be of compact and contiguous territory. The state shall be apportioned into senatorial and representative districts on the basis of population. The general assembly may provide by law for factors in addition to population, not in conflict with the Constitution of the United States, which may be considered in the apportioning of senatorial districts. No law so adopted shall permit the establishment of senatorial districts whereby a majority of the members of the senate shall represent less than forty percent of the population of the state as shown by the most recent United States decennial census.

Section 35. Senators and Representatives--Number and Districts

The general assembly shall in 1971 and in each year immediately following the United States decennial census determine the number of senators and representatives to be elected to the general assembly and establish senatorial and representative districts. The general assembly shall complete the apportionment prior to September 1 of the year so required. If the apportionment fails to become law prior to September 15 of such year, the supreme court shall cause the state to be apportioned into senatorial and representative districts to comply with the requirements of the constitution prior to December 31 of such year. The reapportioning authority shall, where necessary in establishing senatorial districts, shorten the term of any senator prior to completion of the term. Any senator whose term is so terminated shall not be compensated for the uncompleted part of the term.

Section 36. Review by Supreme Court

Upon verified application by any qualified elector, the supreme court shall review an apportionment plan adopted by the general assembly which has been enacted into law. Should the supreme court determine such plan does not comply with the requirements of the constitution, the court shall within ninety days adopt or cause to be adopted an apportionment plan which shall so comply. The supreme court shall have original jurisdiction of all litigation questioning the apportionment of the general assembly or any apportionment plan adopted by the general assembly.

Section 37. Congressional Districts

When a congressional district is composed of two or more counties it shall not be entirely separated by a county belonging to another district and no county shall be divided in forming a congressional district.

Section 38. Elections by General Assembly

In all elections by the general assembly, the members thereof shall vote viva voce and the votes shall be entered on the journal.

Section 38A. Municipal Home Rule

Municipal corporations are granted home rule power and authority, not inconsistent with the laws of the general assembly, to determine their local affairs and government, except that they shall not have power to levy any tax unless expressly authorized by the general assembly.

The rule or proposition of law that a municipal corporation possesses and can exercise only those powers granted in express words is not a part of the law of this state.

Section 39. Legislative Districts

In establishing senatorial and representative districts, the state shall be divided into as many senatorial districts as there are members of the senate and into as many representative districts as there are members of the house of representatives. One senator shall be elected from each senatorial district and one representative shall be elected from each representative district.

Section 39A. Counties Home Rule

Counties or joint county-municipal corporation governments are granted home rule power and authority, not inconsistent with the laws of the general assembly, to determine their local affairs and government, except that they shall not have power to levy any tax unless expressly authorized by the general assembly. The general assembly may provide for the creation and dissolution of joint county-municipal corporation governments. The general assembly may provide for the establishment of charters in county or joint-municipal corporation governments.

If the power or authority of a county conflicts with the power and authority of a municipal corporation, the power and authority exercised by a municipal corporation shall prevail within its jurisdiction.

The proposition or rule of law that a county or joint county-municipal corporation government possesses and can exercise only those powers granted in express words is not a part of the law of this state.

Section 40. Nullification of Administrative Rules

The general assembly may nullify an adopted administrative rule of a state agency by the passage of a resolution by a majority of all of the members of each house of the general assembly.

ARTICLE IV: EXECUTIVE DEPARTMENT

Section 1. Governor

The supreme executive power of this state shall be vested in a chief magistrate, who shall be styled the governor of the state of Iowa.

Section 2. Election and Term

The governor and the lieutenant governor shall be elected by the qualified electors at the time and place of voting for members of the general assembly. Each of them shall hold office for four years from the time of installation in office and until a successor is elected and qualifies.

Section 3. Governor and Lieutenant Governor Elected Jointly--Returns of Elections

The electors shall designate their selections for governor and lieutenant governor as if these two offices were one and the same. The names of nominees for the governor and the lieutenant governor shall be grouped together in a set on the ballot according to which nominee for governor is seeking office with which nominee for lieutenant governor, as prescribed by law. An elector shall cast only one vote for both a nominee for governor and a nominee for lieutenant governor. The returns of every election for governor and lieutenant governor shall be sealed and transmitted to the seat of government of the state, and directed to the speaker of the house of representatives who shall open and publish them in the presence of both houses of the general assembly.

Section 4. Election by General Assembly in Case of Tie-- Succession by Lieutenant Governor

The nominees for governor and lieutenant governor jointly having the highest number of votes cast for them shall be declared duly elected. If two or more sets of nominees for governor and lieutenant governor have an equal and the highest number of votes for the offices jointly, the general assembly shall by joint vote proceed, as soon as is possible, to elect one set of nominees for governor and lieutenant governor. If, upon the completion by the general assembly of the canvass of votes for governor and lieutenant governor, it appears that the nominee for governor in the set of nominees for governor and lieutenant governor receiving the highest number of votes has since died or resigned, is unable to qualify, fails to qualify, or is for any other reason unable to assume the duties of the office of governor for the ensuing term, the powers and duties shall devolve to the nominee for lieutenant governor of the same set of nominees for governor and lieutenant governor, who shall assume the powers and duties of governor upon inauguration and until the disability is removed. If both nominees for governor and lieutenant governor are unable to assume the duties of the office of governor, the person next in succession shall act as governor.

Section 5. Contested Elections

Contested elections for the offices of governor and lieutenant governor shall be determined by the general assembly as prescribed by law.

Section 6. Eligibility

No person shall be eligible to the office of governor, or lieutenant governor, who shall not have been a citizen of the United States, and a resident of the state, two years next preceding the election, and attained the age of thirty years at the time of said election.

Section 7. Commander in Chief

The governor shall be commander in chief of the militia, the army, and navy of this state.

Section 8. Duties of Governor

He shall transact all executive business with the officers of government, civil and military, and may require information in writing from the officers of the executive department upon any subject relating to the duties of their respective offices.

Section 9. Execution of Laws

He shall take care that the laws are faithfully executed.

Section 10. Vacancies

When any office shall, from any cause, become vacant, and no mode is provided by the constitution and laws for filling such vacancy, the governor shall have power to fill such vacancy, by granting a commission, which shall expire at the end of the next session of the general assembly, or at the next election by the people.

Section 11. Convening General Assembly

He may, on extraordinary occasions, convene the general assembly by proclamation, and shall state to both houses, when assembled, the purpose for which they shall have been convened

Section 12. Message

He shall communicate, by message, to the general assembly, at every regular session, the condition of the state, and recommend such matters as he shall deem expedient.

Section 13. Adjournments

In case of disagreement between the two houses with respect to the time of adjournment, the governor shall have power to adjourn the general assembly to such time as he may think proper; but no such adjournment shall be beyond the time fixed for the regular meeting of the next general assembly.

Section 14. Disqualification

No persons shall, while holding any office under the authority of the United States, or this state, execute the office of governor, or lieutenant governor, except as hereinafter expressly provided.

Section 15. Terms—Compensation

The official terms of the governor and lieutenant governor shall commence on the Tuesday after the second Monday of January next after their election and shall continue until their successors are elected and qualify. The governor and lieutenant governor shall be paid compensation and expenses as provided by law. The lieutenant governor, while acting as governor, shall be paid the compensation and expenses prescribed for the governor.

Section 16. Pardons—Reprieves—Commutations

The governor shall have power to grant reprieves, commutations and pardons, after conviction, for all offenses except treason and cases of impeachment, subject to such regulations as may be provided by law. Upon conviction for treason, he shall have power to suspend the execution of the sentence until the case shall be reported to the general assembly at its next meeting, when the general assembly shall either grant a pardon, commute the sentence, direct the execution of the sentence, or grant a further reprieve. He shall have power to remit fines and forfeitures, under such regulations as may be prescribed by law; and shall report to the general assembly, at its next meeting, each case of reprieve, commutation, or pardon granted, and the reasons therefore; and also all persons in whose favor remission of fines and forfeitures shall have been made, and the several amounts remitted.

Section 17. Lieutenant Governor to Act as Governor

In case of the death, impeachment, resignation, removal from office, or other disability of the governor, the powers and duties of the office for the residue of the term, or until he shall be acquitted, or the disability removed, shall devolve upon the lieutenant governor.

Section 18. Duties of Lieutenant Governor

The lieutenant governor shall have the duties provided by law and those duties of the governor assigned to the lieutenant governor by the governor.

Section 19. Succession to Office of Governor and Lieutenant Governor

If there be a vacancy in the office of the governor and the lieutenant governor shall by reason of death, impeachment, resignation, removal from office, or other disability become incapable of performing the duties pertaining to the office of governor, the president of the senate shall act as governor until the vacancy is filled or the disability removed; and if the president of the senate, for any of the above causes, shall be incapable of performing the duties pertaining to the office of governor the same shall devolve upon the speaker of the house of representatives; and if the speaker of the house of representatives, for any of the above causes, shall be incapable of performing the duties of the office of governor, the justices of the supreme court shall convene the general assembly by proclamation and the general assembly shall organize by the election of a president by the senate and a speaker by the house of representatives. The general assembly shall thereupon immediately proceed to the election of a governor and lieutenant governor in joint convention.

Section 20. Seal of State

There shall be a seal of this state, which shall be kept by the governor, and used by him officially, and shall be called the Great Seal of the State of Iowa. See chapter 1A of the Code for a description of the great seal of Iowa.

Section 21. Grants and Commissions

All grants and commissions shall be in the name and by the authority of the people of the state of Iowa, sealed with the great seal of the state, signed by the governor, and countersigned by the secretary of state.

Section 22. Secretary—Auditor—Treasurer

A secretary of state, an auditor of state and a treasurer of state shall be elected by the qualified electors at the same time that the governor is elected and for a four-year term commencing on the first day of January next after their election, and they shall perform such duties as may be provided by law.

ARTICLE V: JUDICIAL DEPARTMENT

Section 1. Courts

The judicial power shall be vested in a supreme court, district courts, and such other courts, inferior to the supreme court, as the general assembly may, from time to time, establish.

Section 2. Supreme Court

The supreme court shall consist of three judges, two of whom shall constitute a quorum to hold court.

Section 3. Election of Judges—Term

Repealed

Section 4. Jurisdiction of Supreme Court

The supreme court shall have appellate jurisdiction only in cases in chancery, and shall constitute a court for the correction of errors at law, under such restrictions as the general assembly may, by law, prescribe; and shall have power to issue all writs and process necessary to secure justice to parties, and shall exercise a supervisory and administrative control over all inferior judicial tribunals throughout the state.

Section 5. District Court and Judge

Repealed

Section 6. Jurisdiction of District Court

The district court shall be a court of law and equity, which shall be distinct and separate jurisdictions, and have jurisdiction in civil and criminal matters arising in their respective districts, in such manner as shall be prescribed by law.

Section 7. Conservators of the Peace

The judges of the supreme and district courts shall be conservators of the peace throughout the state.

Section 8. Style of Process

The style of all process shall be, "The State of Iowa," and all prosecutions shall be conducted in the name and by the authority of the same.

Section 9. Salaries

Repealed

Section 10. Judicial Districts

The general assembly may reorganize the judicial districts and increase or diminish the number of districts, or the number of judges of the said court, and may increase the number of judges of the supreme court; but such increase or diminution shall not be more than one district, or one judge of either court, at any one session; and no reorganization of the districts, or diminution of the number of judges, shall have the effect of removing a judge from office. Such reorganization of the districts, or any change in the boundaries thereof, or increase or diminution of the number of judges, shall take place every four years thereafter, if necessary, and at no other time.
At any regular session of the general assembly the state may be divided into the necessary judicial districts for district court purposes, or the said districts may be reorganized and the number of the districts and the judges of said courts increased or diminished; but no reorganization of the districts or diminution of the judges shall have the effect of removing a judge from office.

Section 11. Judges--When Chosen

Repealed

Section 12. Attorney General

The general assembly shall provide, by law, for the election of an attorney general by the people, whose term of office shall be four years, and until his successor is elected and qualifies.

Section 13. District Attorneys

Repealed

Section 14. System of Court Practice

It shall be the duty of the general assembly to provide for the carrying into effect of this article, and to provide for a general system of practice in all the courts of this state.

Section 15. Vacancies in Courts

Vacancies in the supreme court and district court shall be filled by appointment by the governor from lists of nominees submitted by the appropriate judicial nominating commission. Three nominees shall be submitted for each supreme court vacancy, and two nominees shall be submitted for each district court vacancy. If the governor fails for thirty days to make the appointment, it shall be made from such nominees by the chief justice of the supreme court.

Section 16. State and District Nominating Commissions

There shall be a state judicial nominating commission. Such commission shall make nominations to fill vacancies in the supreme court. Until July 4, 1973, and thereafter unless otherwise provided by law, the state judicial nominating commission shall be composed and selected as follows: There shall be not less than three nor more than eight appointive members, as provided by law, and an equal number of elective members on such commission, all of whom shall be electors of the state. The appointive members shall be appointed by the governor subject to confirmation by the senate. The elective members shall be elected by the resident members of the bar of the state. The judge of the supreme court who is senior in length of service on said court, other than the chief justice, shall also be a member of such commission and shall be its chairman.

There shall be a district judicial nominating commission in each judicial district of the state. Such commissions shall make nominations to fill vacancies in the district court within their respective districts. Until July 4, 1973, and thereafter unless otherwise provided by law, district judicial nominating commissions shall be composed and selected as follows: There shall be not less than three nor more than six appointive members, as provided by law, and an equal number of elective members on each such commission, all of whom shall be electors of the district. The appointive members shall be appointed by the governor. The elective members shall be elected by the resident members of the bar of the district. The district judge of such district who is senior in length of service shall also be a member of such commission and shall be its chairman.

Due consideration shall be given to area representation in the appointment and election of judicial nominating commission members. Appointive and elective members of judicial nominating commissions shall serve for six-year terms, shall be ineligible for a second six-year term on the same commission, shall hold no office of profit of the United States or of the state during their terms, shall be chosen without reference to political affiliation, and shall have such other qualifications as may be prescribed by law. As near as may be, the terms of one-third of such members shall expire every two years.

Section 17. Terms-Judicial Elections

Members of all courts shall have such tenure in office as may be fixed by law, but terms of supreme court judges shall be not less than eight years and terms of district court judges shall be not less than six years. Judges shall serve for one year after appointment and until the first day of January following the next judicial election after the expiration of such year. They shall at such judicial election stand for retention in office on a separate ballot which shall submit the question of whether such judge shall be retained in office for the tenure prescribed for such office and when such tenure is a term of years, on their request, they shall, at the judicial election next before the end of each term, stand again for retention on such ballot. Present supreme court and district court judges, at the expiration of their respective terms, may be retained in office in like manner for the tenure prescribed for such office. The general assembly shall prescribe the time for holding judicial elections.

Section 18. Salaries—Qualifications—Retirement

Judges of the supreme court and district court shall receive salaries from the state, shall be members of the bar of the state and shall have such other qualifications as may be prescribed by law. Judges of the supreme court and district court shall be ineligible to any other office of the state while serving on said court and for two years thereafter, except that district judges shall be eligible to the office of supreme court judge. Other judicial officers shall be selected in such manner and shall have such tenure, compensation and other qualification as may be fixed by law. The general assembly shall prescribe mandatory retirement for judges of the supreme court and district court at a specified age and shall provide for adequate retirement compensation. Retired judges may be subject to special assignment to temporary judicial duties by the supreme court, as provided by law.

Section 19. Retirement and Discipline of Judges

In addition to the legislative power of impeachment of judges as set forth in article three (III), sections nineteen (19) and twenty (20) of the constitution, the supreme court shall have power to retire judges for disability and to discipline or remove them for good cause, upon application by a commission on judicial qualifications. The general assembly shall provide by law for the implementation of this section.

ARTICLE VI: MILITIA

Section 1. Composition—Training

The militia of this state shall be composed of all able-bodied male citizens, between the ages of eighteen and forty-five years, except such as are or may hereafter be exempt by the laws of the United States, or of this state, and shall be armed, equipped, and trained, as the general assembly may provide by law.

Section 2. Exemption

No person or persons conscientiously scrupulous of bearing arms shall be compelled to do military duty in time of peace: Provided, that such person or persons shall pay an equivalent for such exemption in the same manner as other citizens.

Section 3. Officers

All commissioned officers of the militia, (staff officers excepted,) shall be elected by the persons liable to perform military duty, and shall be commissioned by the governor.

ARTICLE VII: STATE DEBTS

Section 1. Credit Not to Be Loaned

The credit of the state shall not, in any manner, be given or loaned to, or in aid of, any individual, association, or corporation; and the state shall never assume, or become responsible for, the debts or liabilities of any individual, association, or corporation, unless incurred in time of war for the benefit of the state.

Section 2. Limitation

The state may contract debts to supply casual deficits or failures in revenues, or to meet expenses not otherwise provided for; but the aggregate amount of such debts, direct and contingent, whether contracted by virtue of one or more acts of the general assembly, or at different periods of time, shall never exceed the sum of two hundred and fifty thousand dollars; and the money arising from the creation of such debts, shall be applied to the purpose for which it was obtained, or to repay the debts so contracted, and to no other purpose whatever.

Section 3. Losses to School Funds

All losses to the permanent, school, or university fund of this state, which shall have been occasioned by the defalcation, mismanagement or fraud of the agents or officers controlling and managing the same, shall be audited by the proper authorities of the state. The amount so audited shall be a permanent funded debt against the state, in favor of the respective fund, sustaining the loss, upon which not less than six per cent. annual interest shall be paid. The amount of liability so created shall not be counted as a part of the indebtedness authorized by the second section of this article.

Section 4. War Debts

In addition to the above limited power to contract debts, the state may contract debts to repel invasion, suppress insurrection, or defend the state in war; but the money arising from the debts so contracted shall be applied to the purpose for which it was raised, or to repay such debts, and to no other purpose whatever.

Section 5. Contracting Debt--Submission to the People

Except the debts herein before specified in this article, no debt shall be hereafter contracted by, or on behalf of this state, unless such debt shall be authorized by some law for some single work or object, to be distinctly specified therein; and such law shall impose and provide for the collection of a direct annual tax, sufficient to pay the interest on such debt, as it falls due, and also to pay and discharge the principal of such debt, within twenty years from the time of the contracting thereof; but no such law shall take effect until at a general election it shall have been submitted to the people, and have received a majority of all the votes cast for and against it at such election; and all money raised by authority of such law, shall be applied only to the specific object therein stated, or to the payment of the debt created thereby; and such law shall be published in at least one newspaper in each county, if one is published therein, throughout the state, for three months preceding the election at which it is submitted to the people.

Section 6. Legislature May Repeal

The legislature may, at any time, after the approval of such law by the people, if no debt shall have been contracted in pursuance thereof, repeal the same; and may, at any time, forbid the contracting of any further debt, or liability, under such law; but the tax imposed by such law, in proportion to the debt or liability, which may have been contracted in pursuance thereof, shall remain in force and be irrepealable, and be annually collected, until the principal and interest are fully paid.

Section 7. Tax Imposed Distinctly Stated

Every law which imposes, continues, or revives a tax, shall distinctly state the tax, and the object to which it is to be applied; and it shall not be sufficient to refer to any other law to fix such tax or object.

Section 8. Motor Vehicle Fees and Fuel Taxes

All motor vehicle registration fees and all licenses and excise taxes on motor vehicle fuel, except cost of administration, shall be used exclusively for the construction, maintenance and supervision of the public highways exclusively within the state or for the payment of bonds issued or to be issued for the construction of such public highways and the payment of interest on such bonds.

Section 9. Fish and Wildlife Protection Funds

All revenue derived from state license fees for hunting, fishing, and trapping, and all state funds appropriated for, and federal or private funds received by the state for, the regulation or advancement of hunting , fishing, or trapping, or the protection, propagation, restoration, management, or harvest of fish or wildlife, shall be used exclusively for the performance and administration of activities related to those purposes.

Section 10. Natural Resources and Outdoor Recreation Trust Fund

A natural resources and outdoor recreation trust fund is created within the treasury for the purposes of protecting and enhancing water quality and natural areas in this State including parks, trails, and fish and wildlife habitat, and conserving agricultural soils in this State. Moneys in the fund shall be exclusively appropriated by law for these purposes.

The General Assembly shall provide by law for the implementation of this section, including by providing for the administration of the fund and at least annual audits of the fund. Except as otherwise provided in this section, the fund shall be annually credited with an amount equal to the amount generated by a sales tax rate of three=eighths of one percent as may be imposed upon the retail sales price of tangible personal property and the furnishing of enumerated services sold in this State.
No revenue shall be credited to the fund until the tax rate for the sales tax imposed upon the retail sales price of tangible personal property and the furnishing of enumerated services sold in this State in effect on the effective date of this section is increased. After such an increased tax rate becomes effective, an amount equal to the amount generated by the increase in the tax rate shall be annually credited to the fund, not to exceed an amount equal to the amount generated by a tax rate of three-eighths of one percent imposed upon the retail sales price of tangible personal property and the furnishing of enumerated services sold in this State.

ARTICLE VIII: CORPORATIONS

Section 1. How Created

No corporation shall be created by special laws; but the general assembly shall provide, by general laws, for the organization of all corporations hereafter to be created, except as hereinafter provided.

Section 2. Taxation of Corporations

The property of all corporations for pecuniary profit, shall be subject to taxation, the same as that of individuals.

Section 3. State Not to Be a Stockholder

The state shall not become a stockholder in any corporation, nor shall it assume or pay the debt or liability of any corporation, unless incurred in time of war for the benefit of the state.

Section 4. Municipal Corporations

No political or municipal corporation shall become a stockholder in any banking corporation, directly or indirectly.

Section 5. Banking Associations

No act of the general assembly, authorizing or creating corporations or associations with banking powers, nor amendments thereto shall take effect, or in any manner be in force, until the same shall have been submitted, separately, to the people, at a general or special election, as provided by law, to be held not less than three months after the passage of the act, and shall have been approved by a majority of all the electors voting for and against it at such election.

Section 6. State Bank

Subject to the provisions of the foregoing section, the general assembly may also provide for the establishment of a state bank with branches.

Section 7. Specie Basis

If a state bank be established, it shall be founded on an actual specie basis, and the branches shall be mutually responsible for each other's liabilities upon all notes, bills, and other issues intended for circulation as money.

Section 8. General Banking Law

If a general banking law shall be enacted, it shall provide for the registry and countersigning, by an officer of state, of all bills, or paper credit designed to circulate as money, and require security to the full amount thereof, to be deposited with the state treasurer, in United States stocks, or in interest paying stocks of states in good credit and standing, to be rated at ten per cent. below their average value in the city of New York, for the thirty days next preceding their deposit; and in case of a depreciation of any portion of said stocks, to the amount of ten per cent. on the dollar, the bank or banks owning such stock shall be required to make up said deficiency by depositing additional stocks: and said law shall also provide for the recording of the names of all stockholders in such corporations, the amount of stock held by each, the time of any transfer, and to whom.

Section 9. Stockholders' Responsibility

Every stockholder in a banking corporation or institution shall be individually responsible and liable to its creditors, over and above the amount of stock by him or her held, to an amount equal to his or her respective shares so held for all of its liabilities, accruing while he or she remains such stockholder.

Section 10. Billholders Preferred

In case of the insolvency of any banking institution, the billholders shall have a preference over its other creditors.

Section 11. Specie Payments—Suspension

The suspension of specie payments by banking institutions shall never be permitted or sanctioned.

Section 12. Amendment or Repeal of Laws--Exclusive Privileges

Subject to the provisions of this article, the general assembly shall have power to amend or repeal all laws for the organization or creation of corporations, or granting of special or exclusive privileges or immunities, by a vote of two thirds of each branch of the general assembly; and no exclusive privileges, except as in this article provided, shall ever be granted.

ARTICLE IX: EDUCATION AND SCHOOL LANDS

Part 1: Education and School Lands:

Section 1. Board of education

The educational interest of the State, including Common Schools and other educational institutions, shall be under the management of a Board of Education, which shall consist of the Lieutenant Governor, who shall be the presiding officer of the Board, and have the casting vote in case of a tie, and one member to be elected from each judicial district in the State.

Section 2. Eligibility

No person shall be eligible as a member of said Board who shall not have attained the age of twenty five years, and shall have been one year a citizen of the State.

Section 3. Election of members

One member of said Board shall be chosen by the qualified electors of each district, and shall hold the office for the term of four years, and until his successor is elected and qualified. After the first election under this Constitution, the Board shall be divided, as nearly as practicable, into two equal classes, and the seats of the first class shall be vacated after the expiration of two years; and one half of the Board shall be chosen every two years thereafter.

Section 4. First session

The first session of the Board of Education shall be held at the Seat of Government, on the first Monday of December, after their election; after which the General Assembly may fix the time and place of meeting.

Section 5. Limitation of sessions

The session of the Board shall be limited to twenty days, and but one session shall be held in any one year, except upon extraordinary occasions, when, upon the recommendation of two thirds of the Board, the Governor may order a special session.

Section 6. Secretary

The Board of Education shall appoint a Secretary, who shall be the executive officer of the Board, and perform such duties as may be imposed upon him by the Board, and the laws of the State. They shall keep a journal of their proceedings, which shall be published and distributed in the same manner as the journals of the General Assembly.

Section 7. Rules and regulations

All rules and regulations made by the Board shall be published and distributed to the several Counties, Townships, and School Districts, as may be provided for by the Board, and when so made, published and distributed, they shall have the force and effect of law.

Section 8. Power to legislate

The Board of Education shall have full power and authority to legislate and make all needful rules and regulations in relation to Common Schools, and other education institutions, but are instituted, to receive aid from the School or University fund of this State: but all acts, rules, and regulations of said Board may be altered, amended or repealed by the General Assembly; and when so altered, amended, or repealed they shall not be re-enacted by the Board of Education.

Section 9. Governor ex officio a member

The Governor of the State shall be, ex officio, a member of said Board.

Section 10. Expenses

The board shall have no power to levy taxes, or make appropriations of money. Their contingent expenses shall be provided for by the General Assembly.

Section 11. State university

The State University shall be established at one place without branches at any other place, and the University fund shall be applied to that Institution and no other.

Section 12. Common schools

The Board of Education shall provide for the education of all the youths of the State, through a system of Common Schools and such school shall be organized and kept in each school district at least three months in each year. Any district failing, for two consecutive years, to organize and keep up a school as aforesaid may be deprived of their portion of the school fund.

Section 13. Compensation

The members of the Board of Education shall each receive the same per diem during the time of their session, and mileage going to and returning therefrom, as members of the General Assembly.

Section 14. Quorum-style of acts

A majority of the Board shall constitute a quorum for the transaction of business; but no rule, regulation, or law, for the government of Common Schools or other educational institutions, shall pass without the concurrence of a majority of all the members of the Board, which shall be expressed by the yeas and nays on the final passage. The style of all acts of the Board shall be, Be it enacted by the Board of Education of the State of Iowa.

Section 15. Board May Be Abolished

The general assembly shall have power to abolish or reorganize said board of education, and provide for the educational interest of the state in any other manner that to them shall seem best and proper.

Part 2: School Funds and School Lands

Section 1. Control—Management

The educational and school funds and lands shall be under the control and management of the general assembly of this state.

Section 2. Permanent Fund

The university lands, and the proceeds thereof, and all monies belonging to said fund shall be a permanent fund for the sole use of the state university. The interest arising from the same shall be annually appropriated for the support and benefit of said university.

Section 3. Perpetual Support Fund

The general assembly shall encourage, by all suitable means, the promotion of intellectual, scientific, moral, and agricultural improvement. The proceeds of all lands that have been, or hereafter may be, granted by the United States to this state, for the support of schools, which may have been or shall hereafter be sold, or disposed of, and the five hundred thousand acres of land granted to the new states, under an act of congress, distributing the proceeds of the public lands among the several states of the union, approved in the year of our Lord one thousand eight hundred and forty-one, and all estates of deceased persons who may have died without leaving a will or heir, and also such percent as has been or may hereafter be granted by congress, on the sale of lands in this state, shall be, and remain a perpetual fund, the interest of which, together with all rents of the unsold lands, and such other means as the general assembly may provide, shall be inviolably appropriated to the support of common schools throughout the state.

Section 4. Fines--How Appropriated

Repealed.

Section 5. Proceeds of Lands

The general assembly shall take measures for the protection, improvement, or other disposition of such lands as have been, or may hereafter be reserved, or granted by the United States, or any person or persons, to this state, for the use of the university, and the funds accruing from the rents or sale of such lands, or from any other source for the purpose aforesaid, shall be, and remain, a permanent fund, the interest of which shall be applied to the support of said university, for the promotion of literature, the arts and sciences, as may be authorized by the terms of such grant. And it shall be the duty of the general assembly as soon as may be, to provide effectual means for the improvement and permanent security of the funds of said university.

Section 6. Agents of School Funds

The financial agents of the school funds shall be the same, that by law, receive and control the state and county revenue for other civil purposes, under such regulations as may be provided by law.

Section 7. Distribution

Repealed

ARTICLE X: AMENDMENTS TO THE CONSTITUTION

Section 1. How proposed—submission

Any amendment or amendments to this constitution may be proposed in either house of the general assembly; and if the same shall be agreed to by a majority of the members elected to each of the two houses, such proposed amendment shall be entered on their journals, with the yeas and nays taken thereon, and referred to the legislature to be chosen at the next general election, and shall be published, as provided by law, for three months previous to the time of making such choice; and if, in the general assembly so next chosen as aforesaid, such proposed amendment or amendments shall be agreed to, by a majority of all the members elected to each house, then it shall be the duty of the general assembly to submit such proposed amendment or amendments to the people, in such manner, and at such time as the general assembly shall provide; and if the people shall approve and ratify such amendment or amendments, by a majority of the electors qualified to vote for members of the general assembly, voting thereon, such amendment or amendments shall become a part of the constitution of this state.

Section 2. More than one amendment

If two or more amendments shall be submitted at the same time, they shall be submitted in such manner that the electors shall vote for or against each of such amendments separately.

Section 3. Constitutional convention

At the general election to be held in the year one thousand nine hundred and seventy, and in each tenth year thereafter, and also at such times as the general assembly may, by law, provide, the question, "Shall there be a convention to revise the constitution, and propose amendment or amendments to same?" shall be decided by the electors qualified to vote for members of the general assembly; and in case a majority of the electors so qualified, voting at such election, for and against such proposition, shall decide in favor of a convention for such purpose, the general assembly, at its next session, shall provide by law for the election of delegates to such convention, and for submitting the results of said convention to the people, in such manner and at such time as the general assembly shall provide; and if the people shall approve and ratify such amendment or amendments, by a majority of the electors qualified to vote for members of the general assembly, voting thereon, such amendment or amendments shall become a part of the constitution of this state. If two or more amendments shall be submitted at the same time, they shall be submitted in such a manner that electors may vote for or against each such amendment separately.

Article XI: Miscellaneous

Section 1. Justice of Peace—Jurisdiction

The jurisdiction of justices of the peace shall extend to all civil cases, (except cases in chancery, and cases where the question of title to real estate may arise,) where the amount in controversy does not exceed one hundred dollars, and by the consent of parties may be extended to any amount not exceeding three hundred dollars.

Section 2. Counties

No new county shall be hereafter created containing less than four hundred and thirty two square miles; nor shall the territory of any organized county be reduced below that area; except the county of Worth, and the counties west of it, along the northern boundary of this state, may be organized without additional territory.

Section 3. Indebtedness of Political or Municipal Corporations

No county, or other political or municipal corporation shall be allowed to become indebted in any manner, or for any purpose, to an amount, in the aggregate, exceeding five per centum on the value of the taxable property within such county or corporation--to be ascertained by the last state and county tax lists, previous to the incurring of such indebtedness.

Section 4. Boundaries of State

The boundaries of the state may be enlarged, with the consent of congress and the general assembly.

Section 5. Oath of Office

Every person elected or appointed to any office, shall, before entering upon the duties thereof, take an oath or affirmation to support the constitution of the United States, and of this state, and also an oath of office.

Section 6. How Vacancies Filled

In all cases of elections to fill vacancies in office occurring before the expiration of a full term, the person so elected shall hold for the residue of the unexpired term; and all persons appointed to fill vacancies in office, shall hold until the next general election, and until their successors are elected and qualified.

Section 7. Land Grants Located

The general assembly shall not locate any of the public lands, which have been, or may be granted by congress to this state, and the location of which may be given to the general assembly, upon lands actually settled, without the consent of the occupant. The extent of the claim of such occupant, so exempted, shall not exceed three hundred and twenty acres.

Section 8. Seat of Government Established--State University

The seat of government is hereby permanently established, as now fixed by law, at the city of Des Moines, in the county of Polk; and the state university, at Iowa City, in the county of Johnson.

Article XII: Schedule

Section 1. Supreme law-constitutionality of acts

This Constitution shall be the supreme law of the State, and any law inconsistent there with, shall be void. The General Assembly shall pass all laws necessary to carry this Constitution into effect. Laws in force.

Section 2 Laws in Force

All laws now in force and not inconsistent with this Constitution, shall remain in force until they shall expire or be repealed.

Section 3. Proceedings not affected

All indictments, prosecutions, suits, pleas, plaints, process, and other proceedings pending in any of the courts, shall be prosecuted to final judgment and execution; and all appeals, writs of error, certiorari, and injunctions, shall be carried on in the several courts, in the same manner as now provided by law; and all offences, misdemeanors, and crimes that may have been committed before the taking effect of this Constitution, shall be subject to indictment, trial and punishment, in the same manner as they would have been, had not this Constitution been made.

Section 4. Fines inure to the state (REPEALED)

All fines, penalties, or forfeitures due, or to become due, or accruing to the State, or to any County therein, or to the school fund, shall inure to the State, county, or school fund, in the manner prescribed by law.

Section 5. Bonds in force

All bonds executed to the State, or to any officer in his official capacity, shall remain in force and inure to the use of those concerned.

Section 6. First election for governor and lieutenant governor

The first election under this Constitution shall be held of the second Tuesday in October, in the year one thousand eight hundred and fifty seven, at which time the electors of the State shall elect the Governor and Lieutenant Governor. There shall also be elected at such election, the successors of such State Senators as were elected at the August election, in the year one thousand eight hundred and fifty-four, and members of the House of Representatives, who shall be elected in accordance with the act of apportionment, enacted at the session of the General Assembly which commenced on the first Monday of December One thousand eight hundred and fifty six.

Section 7. First election of officers

The first election for Secretary, Auditor, and Treasurer of State, Attorney General, District Judges, Members of the Board of Education, District Attorneys, members of Congress and such State officers as shall be elected at the April election, in the year One thousand eight hundred and fifty seven, (except the Superintendent of Public Instruction,) and such county officers as were elected at the August election, in the year One thousand eight hundred and fifty-six, except Prosecuting Attorneys, shall be held on the second Tuesday of October, One thousand eight hundred and fifty-eight: Provided, That the time for which any District Judge or other State or County officer elected at the April election in the year One thousand eight hundred and fifty eight, shall not extend beyond the time fixed for filling like offices at the October election in the year one thousand eight hundred and fifty eight.

Section 8. For judges of supreme court

The first election for Judges of the Supreme Court, and such County officers as shall be elected at the August election, in the year one thousand eight hundred and fifty-seven, shall be held on the second Tuesday of October in the year One thousand eight hundred and fifty-nine.

Section 9. General assembly-first session

The first regular session of the General Assembly shall be held in the year One thousand eight hundred and fifty- eight, commencing on the second Monday of January of said year.

Section 10. Senators

Senators elected at the August election, in the year one thousand eight hundred and fifty-six, shall continue in office until the second Tuesday of October, in the year one thousand eight hundred and fifty nine, at which time their successors shall be elected as may be prescribed by law.

Section 11. Offices not vacated

Every person elected by popular vote, by vote of the General Assembly, or who may hold office by executive appointment, which office is continued by this Constitution, and every person who shall be so elected or appointed, to any such office, before the taking effect of this constitution, (except as in this Constitution otherwise provided,) shall continue in office until the term for which such person has been or may be elected or appointed shall expire: but no such person shall continue in office after the taking effect of this Constitution, for a longer period than the term of such office, in this Constitution prescribed.

Section 12. Judicial districts

The General Assembly, at the first session under this Constitution, shall district the State into eleven Judicial Districts, for District Court purposes; and shall also provide for the apportionment of the members of the General Assembly, in accordance with the provisions of this Constitution.

Submission of constitution. Section 13. This Constitution shall be submitted to the electors of the State at the August election, in the year one thousand eight hundred and fifty-seven, in the several election districts in this State. The ballots at such election shall be written or printed as follows:

Those in favor of the Constitution, New Constitution - Yes.

Those against the Constitution, New Constitution - No.

The election shall be conducted in the same manner as the general elections of the State, and the poll-books shall be returned and canvassed as provided in the twenty-fifth chapter of the code, and abstracts shall be forwarded to the Secretary of State, which abstracts shall be canvassed in the manner provided for in the canvass of State officers.

And if it shall appear that a majority of all the votes cast at such election for and against this Constitution are in favor of the same, the Governor shall immediately issue his proclamation stating that fact, and such Constitution shall be the Constitution of the State of Iowa, and shall take effect from and after the publication of said proclamation.

Proposition to strike out the word "white". Section 14. At the same election that this Constitution is submitted to the people for its adoption or rejection, a proposition to amend the same by striking out the word White from the article on the Right of Suffrage, shall be separately submitted to the electors of this State for adoption or rejection in manner following - Namely:

A separate ballot may be given by every person having a right to vote at said election, to be deposited in a separate box; and those given for the adoption of such proposition shall have the words,

Shall the word White be stricken out of the Article on the Right of Suffrage? Yes.

And those given against the proposition shall have the words, Shall the word White be stricken out of the Article on the Right of Suffrage? No.

And if at said election the number of ballots cast in favor of said proposition shall be equal to a majority of those cast for and against this Constitution, then said word White shall be stricken from said Article and be no part thereof.

Mills county. Section 15.

Until otherwise directed by law, the County of Mills shall be in and a part of the sixth Judicial District of this State.

Done in Convention at Iowa City, this fifth day of March in the year of our Lord One thousand eight hundred and fifty seven, and of the Independence of the United States of America, the eighty first.

In testimony whereof we have hereunto subscribed our names:

TIMOTHY DAY
SHELDON G. WINCHESTER
DAVID BUNKER
D. P. PALMER
GEORGE W. ELLS
J. C. HALL
JOHN H. PETERS
WILLIAM A. WARREN
HOSEA W. GRAY
ROBERT GOWER
H. D. GIBSON
THOMAS SEELY
A. H. MARVIN
J. H. EMERSON

RUFUS L. B. CLARKE
JAMES A. YOUNG
DANIEL H. SOLOMON
M. W. ROBINSON
LEWIS TODHUNTER
JOHN EDWARDS
J. C. TRAER
JAMES F. WILSON
AMOS HARRIS
JOHN T. CLARK
SQUIRE AYERS
HARVEY J. SKIFF
J. A. PARVIN
W. PENN CLARKE
JEREMIAH HOLLINGSWORTH
WILLIAM PATTERSON
DANIEL W. PRICE
ALPHEUS SCOTT
GEORGE GILLASPY
EDWARD JOHNSTONE
AYLETT R. COTTON
FRANCIS SPRINGER, President

Attest:

THOMAS J. SAUNDERS, Secretary
ELLSWORTH N. BATES, Asst. Secretary

PROCLAMATION

Whereas an instrument known as the "New Constitution of the State of Iowa" adopted by the constitutional convention of said State on the fifth day of March A.D. 1857 was submitted to the qualified electors of said State at the annual election held on Monday the third day of August 1857 for their approval or rejection.
And whereas an official canvass of the votes cast at said election shows that there were Forty thousand three hundred and eleven votes cast for the adoption of said Constitution and Thirty eight thousand six hundred and eighty-one votes were cast against its adoption, leaving a majority of sixteen hundred and thirty votes in favor of its adoption.

Now therefore I, JAMES W. GRIMES, Governor of said State, by virtue of the authority conferred upon me, hereby declare that said New Constitution to be adopted, and declare it to be the supreme law of the State of Iowa.
In the testimony whereof I have hereunto set my hand and affixed the Great Seal of the State of Iowa.
L.S. Done at Iowa City this Third day of September A.D. 1857 of the Independence of the United States the eighty second and of the State of Iowa the eleventh.

JAMES W. GRIMES
By the Governor.
Elijah Sells,
Secretary of State.

www.ingramcontent.com/pod-product-compliance
Lightning Source LLC
Chambersburg PA
CBHW070212230526
45471CB00002B/928